HOPE
AGAINST
HOPE

HOPE
AGAINST
HOPE

JOSHUA CHINTAPALLI
with Paul Chintapalli

HOPE AGAINST HOPE

ISBN: 9798714572784

Printed in the United States of America

This book is dedicated to -

All valiant soldiers who do not give up on
their loved ones.

All those making strides on recovery path.

All mental health advocates, champions,
doctors, nurses and social workers.

Foreword

I first met Paul and Mary Chintapalli at a National Alliance on Mental Illness (NAMI) Family Support Group where I served as a facilitator about 7 years ago. At their first meeting Paul told the group that his son, Joshua, had been committed to a State Psychiatric Hospital in Texas to treat his bi-polar disorder.

I remember being impressed by how knowledgeable Paul was about navigating the local mental health system and how lucky his son Joshua was to have such caring and supportive parents. This is not always the case; some parents in Paul and Mary's situation abandon their children physically and/or emotionally. With extended hospitalization, effective medications, and his parents' full support, Joshua's condition seemed to stabilize, and I believe Paul and Mary thought this nightmare of an illness was all in the past.

About a year later I asked Mary to help with a NAMI advocacy effort in our county. On the long drive to the County Courthouse, Mary told me that Joshua, now in college, had stopped using bi-polar medications, had relapsed, and was using illegal drugs. She then relayed to me the story of how their effort to help their son in a crisis by calling the local police had resulted in a fiasco which put their son in jail for months and caused major damage to their home.

Once Paul sent me the manuscript for this book and I started reading it, I could not put it down. As every parent with a child with a brain disorder knows, helping them cope with their illness and keeping them safe often takes unconditional love to an extreme. That love certainly comes through in this book.

Facing mental illness and/or addiction in your child can be described as "being hit by a Mack truck". It can be devastating. It is so difficult for parents to face the realization that the child that has been the center of their lives and for whom they have so many wonderful hopes and dreams, is no longer the same person they knew;

- that they cannot control another human being or their illness;

- that these biologically based brain disorders, though treatable, are often chronic and may require lifelong attention, medical care, and lifestyle management;

- that their expectations for their child may need to change;

- that they need to set boundaries and find their own coping mechanisms, so that the stress will not destroy them, their marriage, and family;

- that they need to educate themselves about mental illness, addictions and drugs from reliable sources—as the two are often seen together and need to be treated together;

-   and that their child or loved one is not a lost cause and they should never give up hope.

Through Paul and Mary's journey they have learned all these things and more. By revealing their personal story with their son and hearing directly from Joshua about experiencing the mental illness, which first manifested its symptoms in adolescence with risky behaviors and heavy drug use to self-medicate, I know they will help many others recognize and face mental illness and/or addiction in their own families and provide them with the wisdom and encouragement to survive this all too common and painfully challenging reality of life.

Joan Abrams
NAMI Member,
Former Support Group Facilitator for over two decades

Contents

Preface

One nightmare for anyone is to deal with their loved ones addicted to drugs or alcohol, or afflicted with mental illness. There is no telling which one is worse, but the consequences to the immediate family are horrific and traumatic.

I am not sure every addiction or mental illness story ends well, but I want to tell you that there is always a hope if you're an addict or suffering with mental illness. By God's grace and with a loving family standing beside you, you have odds on your side to come out of this mess.

If you're the loved one caring for an addict, or someone with mental illness, in your family, there is hope for you. It is not easy to see it when all you see is destruction and hopelessness in front of you, but there is hope. My own family is first hand witness to this. The outcome may not be to your liking, but one day you would be able to appreciate clinging on to this hope.

My dad and I decided to write this brief personal experience as a story to encourage those who in the midst of this painful journey that one day you too may experience the joy of seeing a resolution.

All the events detailed in this book are factual, but no liability is attributed to any institution or a group, or a person.

We all make mistakes, and some of these mistakes cost us more than what we are willing to pay in terms of consequences, but with love, patience and above all a genuine trust in God's sovereign grace, you can go to the other side.

Acknowledgements

I would like to dedicate this book to those who made wrong choices, and/or suffering with mental illness, but are fighting to get back to normalcy again. Likewise, to all parents, or the loved ones who don't give up, but do their best to affirm love and care for their loved one.

I also dedicate this to NAMI volunteers and coordinators who do their best to help the people on the wrong road, and be a place for the struggling family to express themselves.

To all those who prayed for my well-being earnestly and tried to assure me during my dark days.

My sincere thanks to Collin County Mental Health Authority (CC MHA), Lifepath Systems, for their support during my recovery and on-going support.

To all my family – mom, dad and brother – who showed unflinching love and commitment to help me back on the track. Also, I want to acknowledge many others, especially those who prayed for me earnestly and who stood by me during my progress.

1. INTRODUCTION

Normal human experience is inherently filled with ongoing struggles in so many aspects. Any ill-health in a family, loss of a loved one on a wrong path, compounds the struggles – from stigma to shame, from helplessness to hopelessness.

1.1 Why this book?

This is to share first-hand experience in making wrong choices, facing the terrible consequences and finally turning around towards normal life. This is to encourage those who are involved in any addiction, drugs or alcohol, that there is a way to get out of the rut, at least to certain point of normal function.

It is a true story of a young man (Joshua, the author) whose life is turned upside down due to drug addiction before it turned around for good, with treatment for underlying mental illness, despite so many setbacks. Everything documented here is a real-life experience that took place not too long ago, and it is an ongoing journey.

It is the story of a father (Paul) and a son (Joshua). Paul encouraged Josh to openly talk about his destructive path to those who are still on that path and what it cost him. Perhaps it may encourage some of them to reconsider their choices. It is also to show them that they can get well with the help of the family who standby them.

It is also the story of a father who walked down this path in dealing with an addict on a destructive path, but finally able to see light at the end of the tunnel.

Both Josh and Paul narrate their perspectives and struggles walking down this path. There is no sugar coating of the real events that took place over a span of 10+ years.

Josh talks about his path towards drugs and the destructive nature of this journey and struggles with mental illness in chapter II. In chapter III, Paul talks about his challenges, path of hope, and a coping mechanism that helped him persevere during this ordeal. In Chapter IV, Paul talks about lasting hope, something beyond a coping mechanism.

If this book helped you one way or the other, please recommend it to others. It is priced low so you can perhaps buy a few copies and pass them on to those who are in the middle of a struggle.

To protect the people involved, pseudonyms were used unless the person gave permission to use their real name.

We pray and trust that this book offers hope, perseverance and a godly coping mechanism and hope that will help you go to the other side of the struggle. Hope against hope.

2. ADDICTION & CONSEQUENCES

2.1 An addiction - When I realized it

From the beginning of my adolescence, I remember that I've always wanted to rebel against the expectations that my loved ones had for me. I hadn't considered my parents emotions or the consequences that I could face at school. I only thought about the bad things that I could experiment with and all of what life had to offer. I thought that life was about doing drugs, having sex, being rebellious, doing troublesome things and the thrill of getting away with it. However, when there came times where I was caught for my rebellious acts, I still maintained the mindset that doing bad things were worthwhile.

When I was 12 years old, I was indirectly introduced to cigarettes. I watched my father's friend throw cigarette butts outside our front lawn every time he came over. One day as I went to get the mail, I saw that he left a couple of cigarette butts on our front lawn as usual and I decided to pick one up and light it with a birthday candle lighter. I don't remember if I coughed from the cigarette, but I remember that I enjoyed it.

My mom came outside and saw me inhale the cigarette and then screamed at me to put it down and get back inside the home. I anticipated that I would be in trouble. She gave me a firm lecture and told me to never smoke cigarettes again. However, as the rebellious kid that I had been, I completely ignored her and went to a nearby gas station the next day and asked the man behind the counter if I could buy some cigarettes. I'm confident that he was aware that I was underaged, but still sold me a pack of Marlboro 27s.

Several years passed and I was 16 years old in high school, and living it up. I had a girlfriend, lots of friends, bad habits, and a driver's permit. I had a couple of bad friends and plenty of good friends. However, I chose to spend most of my time with the bad friends rather than the good ones. The more time I spent with my bad friends, the more I lost my relationship with my good friends. Everybody could see the horrible choices I was making through my body, my face and especially my demeanor. This was around the time I started doing marijuana.

Marijuana was the main cause of most major problems that I'm still dealing with to this day. Although I quit marijuana use a long time ago, the charges that remain on my record, seeing probation officers every month, and other addictions were the consequences that came along with the marijuana abuse. The propaganda that marijuana users promote that "marijuana isn't a gateway drug" is false from my own personal experience, because marijuana is definitely a gateway drug. I've known many marijuana users that proceeded to do cocaine, heroin, and other hard drugs gradually.

The use of hard drugs should not be taken lightly as they can cause severe consequences if you have mental health disorders similar to myself. At that time, I didn't know I had mental health disorders so I didn't know what the long-term consequences were for me.

Any form of addiction is not an easy thing to cover up if you had a track record of getting caught in your lies and displaying physical and mental changes. If I were put in the position to discern whether an individual abused drugs or not, it would be easier than trying to catch a fly with two hands since drugs have the capability to completely change you into an empty shell of yourself. I remember that my parents would always worry about how my body became so thin and how my lies became so frequent with my drug use. When I began smoking cigarettes, it wasn't easy to get away with because I was underaged and not legally allowed to smoke cigarettes. Although I've come to the legal age to purchase and smoke cigarettes, it's looked down upon by my family. My parents constantly told me that I needed to quit and that I will be able to overcome it.

When I began purchasing cigarettes, I would smoke them far away from my house. I usually would go to some random alleyway because I was afraid that if I smoked the cigarettes on a sidewalk my parents would be driving by and catch me. Then, I would douse myself in some cheap cologne to get rid of the smell and occasionally start chewing some mint gum.

However, I was caught most of the time because I was bad at hiding the smell of my breath and the strong odor it left on my clothes. Cigarettes and marijuana have the strongest smells next to gasoline, so you can imagine why it's so hard to hide the smell even if you were smoking them in an alleyway. To purchase cigarettes before I became of legal age, I would buy them at the local gas station, which later got shut down because of its illegal activities, or get them from my friends at the school.

2.2 Covering up the Addiction

When I was heavily using marijuana, I stumbled upon the same issues of hiding it from my parents as I did with cigarettes. The smell, red eyes, the dreadful anxiety as well as lethargy that came with weed were the hardest to manage when coming back home after an entire day of getting high.

As soon as I came home, my dad could immediately tell I was high because he could smell it on me, saw how red my eyes were, and heard how my voice sounded when I entered the house. No matter how many times I tried to hide the smell in cologne or use eye drops to remedy my red eyes, my father would always be aware of when I was high.

The method that I went to obtain weed was through various drug dealers that would approach me or through my friends. The first time that I ever did weed was with my ex-best friend in 9th grade. We would hang out every day after school at each other's houses and most of the time we would make music, play video games, or go outside and play sports.

One day, a drug dealer approached us and said that he sold weed and it piqued my interest because I've heard people talk about how weed was "fun". I decided to wait until it was night time and I messaged the weed dealer to meet him at a local fast-food restaurant and bought a gram of weed. Then I brought it home to my friend who was sleeping over at my house for the night. We waited until my parents fell asleep and we tried to put the weed in a flower vase as a replacement for a bong and used a lighter.

However, we quickly realized that there's no way that it would possibly work and we thought since people are able to eat weed through brownies and other edibles, we could directly ingest the weed and get high. We proceeded to split the gram of weed in half and ate it. The few hours that we stayed awake after consuming the weed, we didn't feel anything so we ended up falling asleep on the living room couch.

When we both woke up in the morning my friend said he felt like his eyes were rolling to the back of his head, but I still did not feel anything from the weed. When I went to the kitchen to drink some water, I passed out and hit my head on the kitchen floor. My friend immediately went to go find my mom, and she called the ambulance.

I don't remember the ambulance ride to the hospital or being on the hospital bed, but I specifically remember being discharged from the hospital and apologizing to my parents for doing weed behind their back. Despite the apology to my parents, I wanted to continue to use weed discreetly and figure out the methods to properly use it.

A year after my first encounter with the weed, I met Aiden (not real name). Aiden had brought an entire world of pain that continued to affect my life in the long run. I gradually spent more time with Aiden and getting caught up in his shenanigans. It meant spending less time with my old best friend. Whenever I hung out with Aiden after school, we would always get weed from his friends or drug dealers which led us into experimenting with acid. Before we further discuss the experimentation on acid, I want to illustrate a description of what kind of friend Aiden was to me.

Fast forward to when Aiden and I both graduated from high school and enrolled into college.

Around this time, Aiden introduced me to acid and encouraged me to try it in his car with a mutual friend. It felt like we were going in circles with Aiden driving around to go pick up more of our friends to smoke weed and coming back to the same spot. As I felt the effects of acid consuming my body, the hallucinations that I saw throughout the trip were unforgettable.

There were numerous occasions in my adolescence in which my father tried to protect me from danger. However, at that time I considered my father's attempts to protect me as him trying to rain on my parade.

Continuing my marijuana abuse, one day my friends and I gathered together at a friend's house, whom we'll call Gary, to celebrate the stoner's holiday. Before we began longboarding around the neighborhood, my friends and I decided to take an eighth of shrooms each through chocolate bars. As we longboarded, we proceeded rapidly downhill and I couldn't stop myself before I hit the curb that was next to the sidewalk. The shrooms had made it feel like my body floated in the air and landed gracefully, as if I were picked up by angels and gently placed down onto earth. Subsequently I wasn't able to find any of my friends and began to feel perturbed because of the hallucinations caused by shrooms in the form of evil faces twisted onto trees, houses, and everything around me. This caused me to feel terrified.

After what felt like an eternity, my friends pulled up next to me in Gary's truck and drove me back to the friends' house. As I left their truck, I felt exceedingly nauseous and clutched onto the back of the truck before fainting and hitting my head on the street. I bled profusely on the back of my head and my friends rushed me into the house and situated me on the couch, then they forced milk into my mouth to reduce the shrooms effects.

After I recovered from the shrooms, I called my father and explained what happened to me and he came to the house to get me. He didn't seem angry at me, but rather disappointed and was concerned for my well-being.

A couple of days later, I spent another night at Gary's house and my father showed up to figure out what I was doing there again. I told him that he couldn't just barge into another person's home like that and he firmly told me not to do anything stupid again, but come home safe. When he finally left, my friends came to me and asked if I wanted to smoke some weed and I agreed to join them.

As more time passed, Aiden and Gary realized that I was becoming a non-functional stoner and that I couldn't hold conversations so they started becoming better friends with each other than I was with them, even though I introduced them to each other.

The Downward Spiral

Before my friendship with Aiden and Gary completely fell through, we had a "brilliant, but stupid" plan to do mischievous things to get expensive items at our high school and sell them to other students for profit.

I would be the one to get the merchandise and Aiden would be the one to find the students that would purchase the merchandise. It felt as if we had created our own school campus black market. I remember getting a PSP console from a student in our gym class, another student's wallet, and a student's phone as it sat on the table after the teacher told us to hand our phones to him.

However, the student was able to trace down their phone with the "Find My iPhone" application and noticed that it was at my home. The student notified the teacher that promised not to tell the principal as long as I returned the phone to the student. I returned the phone to the student but still kept the other items that I got. Afterwards, we hastily sold those items to students that Aiden was acquainted with and we made a profit.

Eventually, we were caught because we sold the PSP console to a student that reported us and the school authorities pulled me out of orchestra class to interrogate me. The school authorities searched through my phone, backpack, and wallet and found messages from drug dealers and the students that we sold to on my phone.

Shortly, Aiden and I were arrested and when we were placed in the back of the police cruiser, we fist bumped and exclaimed "hell yeah, our first time getting arrested!". We spent the night in a jail cell where we had black coffee, a honeybun, a mattress, a blanket, and a jumpsuit. When we were released, the school suspended us for the rest of the year in a program called ISS and we weren't able to see any of our friends anymore. I came to know later through my dad that Plano PD dropped the charges with a warning so as not to ruin my young life.

The following year I began to spend time with two other male students and a female student during lunch to smoke weed and drink alcohol. We got high instead of eating lunch and the male students would have intercourse with the female student. In one instance, our routine drug dealer couldn't sell us any weed so we went to a sketchy dealer in Dallas and got some laced weed. The others didn't feel the effects from the laced weed but for me it felt like my ears were ringing and I was losing all of my senses. I returned to my science class and the teacher announced that there would be a pop quiz, which heightened my anxiety even more. When I completed the pop quiz, I wasn't able to turn in the assignment because I immediately collapsed into a Grand Mal seizure, which is the worst type of seizure. I remember waking up in the school nurse's office with the worst migraine. It felt as if I got shot through the head with a bullet and survived.

When I returned to school the next day, the teacher told me that I needed to go to the principal's office and the principal suspended me with ISS. I spent the rest of senior year in ISS and made a couple of new friends, one of whom was the popular student that everybody knew and another was a student who liked to get "high" off peppers and made crappy beats on his laptop. When I graduated high school, I did not reminisce on the memories with fondness because I never liked any of the students as much as the other students at the high school that I transferred from.

2.3 Abuse Escalation & California Trip

When I enrolled into college, I continued doing the worst kind of drugs. I maintained one friendship in the senior year of high school with a guy we'll call Aaron that continued throughout college. Initially, Aaron was my acid dealer but began to take advantage of me and had me drive him to deliver acid to his customers. I would constantly trip on acid to the point that I would be on acid during my classes, I didn't have many friends, but it didn't matter to me because I preferred doing acid by myself. I didn't need to hide acid or shrooms from my parents because I would either trip when they were asleep or before I came home from college, additionally there weren't any scents or physical attributes that would need to be disguised.

However, the severe mental changes that I went through weren't easy to hide because the drugs brought my mind to somewhere that would make me do insane stuff. For example, one time I overdosed on K2 (synthetic marijuana).

The time I overdosed on K2 was not a fun memory, mainly because I died and came back to life. Rewind to 2013, when I was working at Subway. When I was working that night at another Subway that my boss owned, a couple of my buddies came to the store to get some free food in exchange for some weed. After I served them up they gave me the weed, or so I thought it was real weed. They decided to wait till I got off my shift to smoke with me since I only had 30 more minutes on the clock. Once I clocked out, my buddy and his friends came to my house.

When we got to my house, we entered inside and saw that my brother was just on his laptop playing in the game room. This is important to note because it shows what really can happen even while a loved one can be a moment's notice away. When I let my buddy's friend roll up the blunt, I thought they used just my weed and their weed. However, this was not the case. When we sparked up the blunt and smoked about half of it, my head started getting really light-headed. Then I felt my life drained out and I collapsed.

During this time, I saw my life flash before my eyes and my soul entering Hell. Meanwhile in the real world, my buddy was trying to resuscitate me by clasping his hands together and pumping on my chest where my heart was. In those few seconds when my heart wasn't beating, I saw demons and people being tortured by the Lake of Fire. Right before my friend's so-called CPR finally worked and brought me back to life, I saw an angel with multiple faces on one head and eyes all over his wings and wearing a white garment coming through a hole at the top to pull me back into my body. When life breathed back into me, I just got up and went inside and all my buddy's friends were gone and the K2 weed was gone too.

After this overdose, I thought that a rapper celebrity was my actual father. Then I decided to drive to California on a full tank of gas and twenty bucks to my pocket. I was only able to travel four hours away from home and ended up in Abilene, TX. I made my way to a semi-truck stop and the sheriff gave me a couple of gallons of gas and sent me on my way. I attempted to drive further towards California and ended up at a chicken restaurant nearby, where I spent the cold night inside my car. I tried to come up with rhymes and lyrics that I would show to the rapper if he came there. I constantly messaged him on social media thinking that it would give him an incentive to come to me. The next morning, I went into the chicken restaurant to use the restroom and then continued on my trip to California.

Instead of driving to California, I ended up traveling to Oklahoma where I stopped at another gas station since I ran out of gas. I sat at the gas station for hours because I had no more money to refill my gas tank and a police officer came to me and asked me why I was still at the gas station. I told the police officer that I ran out of gas and had no money to refill my gas tank, so the police officer kindly offered to refill my gas tank with ten dollars and I started driving towards Abilene again.

2.4 Train Accident & Arrest at Greyhound

By the time I reached Abilene, I took a tab of acid to ease my stress from the rapper celebrity who didn't show up. I became completely non-attentive, recklessly driving down the wrong access road and crashing into a dead end. Somehow, I thought that the dead end meant "Enter Here" so I floored it and tried to return to the highway, but the dead end was a ditch with train tracks in them. I hit the train tracks and the train was about a minute away from reaching me. Since the driver side door was duct taped shut from outside to keep it closed properly, I had to quickly get out from my passenger side. The train came and crashed into my car while I was standing on the side of the ditch.

My mind was blank, I thought if I waited there the rapper would see the incident on the news and come to pick me up. However, five sheriffs came to the site and charged me with public destruction. The incident was broadcast on the local news and a tow truck took my car to the junkyard. That was the end of my first car, a 94 Honda Accord.

Before he went to the junkyard, the tow truck driver dropped me at the Greyhound bus station. I continued on my journey to find my imaginary father, the celebrity rapper. I tried to sneak onto the Greyhound bus without ticket and the bus driver saw me and told me to get off the bus as a warning. However, when I tried to get back on the bus again, the bus driver called the police. I went inside the bus station to pretend to purchase a bus ticket and called my actual father to purchase a bus ticket. He found my location and began to drive there. The police officer came to me and I told the police officer that I'm on acid and confused about why I tried to get onto the Greyhound bus without ticket. The police officer charged me with public intoxication and proceeded to take me to the police station.

My father noticed me talking to the police officer and followed the police car to the police station. He patiently waited at the jail facility the entire night until I was released. When I was released, my father wanted me to get into the car and return home, but I adamantly refused. I waited outside the police station for hours and hours, believing that the rapper celebrity would come and pick me up. By night, I began to walk down the street to find a place of shelter but the places nearby were closed, so I waited on a bench in a store complex. The people leaving the store complex noticed me and asked if I was alright and needed an ambulance.

Still reeling from psychosis, I thought that the people were undercover cops and the ambulance would be going back to the police station, so I declined their offer. When it became too cold, I began to walk again and a police officer stopped me and asked what I was doing out in the freezing cold. I told the police officer that my father was waiting for me, and when the police officer asked for a phone number, I gave him my real father's phone number because I didn't have the celebrity's phone number. My father brought me home after purchasing fast food for me. I thought that the food tasted horrible though but it might have been the acid that made everything taste horrible.

2.5 Rehab & Living through Delusions

There were several incidents tied to drug abuse that eventually got me diagnosed with bipolar illness.

The first mental rehab hospital that I was admitted to gave the patients much more freedom than the other ones that I would be admitted to later on. The patients were allowed to smoke cigarettes at the hospital, the hospital provided snack breaks often, and patients were discharged much earlier than at the other hospital. I was admitted to this particular hospital three times, the reason that I was admitted the first time was because I became manic.

As I continued in my manic state, my father got a mental health warrant from JP court. I remember arriving at the hospital in a police cruiser and walking inside with the police officers. The nurses at the hospital asked me several questions that every mental health patient is asked before being admitted to the hospital, such as "What medications are you on?" and "Do you have suicidal thoughts or thoughts of harming somebody?".

When the nurses asked me for my father's contact information, I told them that my father is the rapper celebrity that I've previously mentioned above and the nurses realized that I was manic and had delusions of grandeur. The nurses put a red band around my wrist for high-risk patients. When the nurses let me inside, I thought that the hospital seemed nice, the beds were made with comfy blankets, patients were eating food in their beds and smoking cigarettes in the smoke room, it seemed more like a cozy social club than a mental rehab facility.

Of course, I had to take my medications routinely and sometimes get an injection if I was acting up to put me to sleep. I used to have conversations with other patients and share my food with them and sometimes go out for smoke breaks when it felt like the medications were messing with my head. I remember the heavy brain fog that I would have and thinking that the rapper celebrity was inside an ambulance because of the nurses saying "He's in the ambulance." I thought that the nurses were referring to the rapper celebrity that was my father in my manic induced mindset. One day, the nurses told me that I would be going to the "other side" and I thought that it meant that I would break free of the shackles of reality and boost myself to the celebrity world, but I realized that the "other side" meant the other side of the hospital.

The other side of the hospital had beds that laid flat on the ground, a large smoke room, and the patients seemed more ill. Most of the patients seemed to either have severe mental issues or were high suicide or homicidal risk. I remember that there was a large TV to watch but whenever I became manic, I didn't care about the TV unless it had rap music playing. I remained on the other side of the hospital for some time until one of the nurses came to talk to me. Because I thought that the nurse was one of the rapper's agents and was sent to interview me, I answered all of her questions as if it was the celebrity talking to me.

At the end of the conversation, I was placed on stricter watch and had a different wristband. The fact that I told the nurse that I wanted to get high every day and wanted to become famous made the nurses realize that I was much more delusional than initially thought. I remained at the other side of the hospital for another week. Then I was released because I didn't have health insurance.

My continued abuse of drugs put me in a manic state often and added trauma to my family. It led me to be admitted at Terrel State Hospital, where I didn't have the delusions of the rapper celebrity being my father. This is where they formally diagnosed my bi-polar and schizophrenia conditions. It was the longest stay, nearly 3+ weeks, through a court order.

When I was admitted into the hospital, I walked from the first building to another one that was across the street, the building was much larger and it felt as if I walked into a recreation center.

I remember that the room had a large TV on the wall with chairs, couches, and a table, and there was another table for arts and crafts at the end of the room. I decided to go to the arts and crafts table and drew a flower to put it in the center of the desk and by the time I finished the drawing, it was time for the patients to get our medications.

During my time at this hospital, I read books more than watching TV and slept often. When my parents came to visit me, they brought a suitcase full of clothes and snacks and I was always so happy to see them because I realized that my parents were always there to support me no matter if I was in jail or the mental hospital.

At one time, I walked past one patient so often that she became irritated and attempted to throw a chair at me and the nurses grabbed the chair from her. The manic episodes became more tolerable when we were able to play sports like basketball or soccer outside. When I played basketball, it would distract my mind from being manic and I would immerse myself in basketball.

One day, I participated in the church session that the hospital held and it brought tears to my eyes because I felt as if God was healing my brain. I had never felt such light in my body before. When the hospital discharged me, my parents came to take me home and I never felt happier to be released from the hospital. The sofas at the hospital were uncomfortable and I thought the food was terrible, so I was happy that I could lounge on comfy couches and eat delicious food at my parents house.

2.6 The Worst Day

Despite the absurd road trip to California, the worst incident happened in October 2015 while I routinely abused acid. It was my first attempt to commit suicide. The acid abuse made such severe changes in my mind that I felt as if I wasn't able to control my actions anymore. I remember taking a steak knife from the kitchen cabinet and telling my parents to leave the house, in an attempt to use it on myself. They were scared and thought I was attempting to harm them so they also took my brother with them.

I barricaded the house and went to my room. I called the police and sent a false alarm that I had bombs, hostages, and guns, when I knew I didn't. The police brought the SWAT team, hostage crisis team, and bomb squad. My parents told the police that I had drug related mental illness, and I only had a steak knife and nothing else. At that point, my goal was to commit suicide by cops shooting at me.

I prepared myself to get shot with bullets, so I wore five layers of clothes and a pillowcase on my head to prevent the tear gas from incapacitating me. I tried to stab myself in the neck with the steak knife to escape the intolerable tear gas, but it didn't pierce through because of the pillowcase on my head. Afterwards, I sat on the floor in front of my closet and waited for the SWAT team to shoot at me. The police broke my bedroom windows and sent a robot to my door and aimed at me with assault rifles, but they didn't use the lethal force that I anticipated. Instead, the SWAT team used rubber bullets on me and tased me.

I don't remember the police taking me to the hospital. I woke up in the hospital bed with metal rods in my right kneecap and a missing knuckle on my left ring finger. The hospital treated me for my injuries before the police escorted me to jail in a wheelchair.

2.7 Second Suicide Attempt

I made another suicide attempt when I flooded the jail cell with sink water and tried plugging my fingers into a wall socket. Obviously, it didn't work because my fingers were too big for the wall socket holes. When the jail cell was cleaned up, they put me back in and I started peeing into cups and throwing it at the jailers when they walked by. I routinely did this for about a week until the warden came to see me. To retaliate, I took a mustard packet and smashed it against the window. The warden told me to back away from the door and proceeded to mace the jail cell. I sat on the metal toilet and grabbed onto the metal handle next to it and waited for them to tase me with a stun gun.

The warden and jailers tased me and riot-shielded me after pepper spraying me. Then they brought me to another jail cell with a table with straps on it. They wrapped the straps around me and one of the jailers that had a riot shield grabbed my jaw and held my head down to prevent me from biting him. They left me in the jail cell for the rest of the day and came to see if I was in better condition the next day. I started crying and promised them that I won't mess with the jailers anymore. Then I felt like I was sent to the coldest cell in the entire jail house. I couldn't see the jailers from the cell and it felt like time was passing by slowly.

The vivid manic episodes continued to persist after the jailers transferred me to the cold cell. For instance, I would routinely strip off my clothes and put them in the toilet and the jailers would tell me to put my clothes back on when they noticed me. Also, I would stand on the bed frame and create soundtracks inspired by Star Wars in my mind and imagine scenarios such as going down to hell and saving my father from being crucified.

One time, the jailers mistakenly left my cell door open after letting me out to shower. Then I snuck out and went to their break room and ate one of the donuts and put a laptop in my jumpsuit. However, they caught me and demanded that I give back the laptop. I thought that they were evil for not allowing any of the inmates to have their donuts, so I convinced myself that they were committing unforgivable crimes against the inmates and I needed to defend them. After one of my showers, I tried to grab onto the jailer's legs and they twisted my hands and put the cuffs on me. I was shaking and writhing while they manhandled me.

After two months of incarceration, I was able to contact my parents and have book privileges. Having conversations with my mother would bring me back to reality more than medication. Another week came by and the warden came to ask if I wanted to be transferred to the general population in jail since my leg seemed to have healed from the knee surgery and I agreed.

During the time that I was in the general population, I constantly screamed at everything so the jailers transferred me back into SHU, which is the isolation unit, but I was released from isolation after 2 weeks of good behavior.

I was in the SHU, Special-Housing-Unit meant primarily for isolating inmates, for 2 weeks in total. I experienced an exorbitant amount of darkness and loneliness there. At certain times it felt like I died and it felt like being in hell. I was unexplainably lonely and stuck in a small room with nobody else to see or hear besides the jailers who I thought were the demons of that hell. For mentally ill people, SHU is a literally hellish experience.

I had vivid manic episodes. In one instance, I thought that I was a Viking fighting dragons with gunships and saving damsels in distress from evil and I also thought I was able to shapeshift.

When I was in the SHU for the first time for about a week I was in a cell where I could see the jailers walk around for the most part and even other inmates standing at their cell window. However, the second time I was in the SHU for another week I was in a cell where I couldn't see the jailers for half the time or the inmates at all. That was when I went explicitly manic-psycho and started tearing up the one book that was in my cell, the Bible. Before I tore it up I would try to read it by flipping it to random pages and would end up landing on Psalm 34 over and over. This drove me insane and I ended up throwing the torn-up pages all over my cell. When I did this, I felt an overwhelming sense of darkness taking over my spirit and mind. This was when I started gutter screaming at the jailers when they passed by as I felt like demons were entering my body and possessing me.

Since then, I have repented for this grave sin I committed. The craziest part after this incident was that a jailer told to me that he was my dad who was shapeshifting to keep me safe. In addition, whenever I took showers and had my 10-minute outside break, I would scream and make a racket to where all the inmates would watch me, but the jailers wouldn't stop me.

While in my cell, I would eat the commissary foods my parents sent me and write plenty of notes or draw. I started feeling normal once they put me on medications. The warden told me they would be releasing me out of the SHU after a week of being there on "good behavior" and back into gen-pop, general population.

I attended the first trial to be released from jail after four months and received 6 years of probation. I learned that if I attended the second trial, I would have been able to receive a lesser probation sentence, but my addiction to nicotine overcame me and I jumped on the chance to be released to smoke cigarettes. When I was released from jail, I immediately went to smoke a cigarette and my parents came to get me. My parents gave a ride to an acquaintance of mine that had been released from jail and my dad bought me a pack of cigarettes before we came home.

My parents informed me that my beloved cat passed away from kidney disease while I was incarcerated. I noticed that the house had new carpets and couches. I learned that the whole house was destroyed when SWAT entered the house and the insurance company fixed it. I felt astonished that so much has changed since my incarceration.

2.8 On the Path towards Recovery

Though I have been sober for the last 5+years, it has not been easy. There were some stumbles along the way due to my negligence and indulgence in unhealthy choices.

From time to time, I was admitted to Methodist Richardson Hospital due to manic relapses. I would stay up at night and watch video game streams, blast metal music, and not on schedule or take medicine as prescribed.

The manic state continued for some time. One morning, I wandered off into our neighborhood with just my boxer shorts only. The police stopped me and called for ambulance when I answered the police absurdly.

I remained at the hospital for some time and my parents came and brought me fast food to eat before they sent me to Methodist rehab building. I remember that I enjoyed the food and talking to the patients, but would continue to be manic and thought that I had superpowers that would send people to the spirit realm. I became friends with almost every patient the second and third time that I went to that hospital. I noticed during my second hospitalization that the patients were allowed to smoke e-cigarettes in the facility.

During the second and third time I went to the mental hospital, I was placed in the isolation room and I would have manic episodes each time. The manic episodes during the third time would cause me to think that I was stuck in space; I thought that I was floating in space and nobody would ever be able to find me, so I wouldn't be discharged from the hospital. I imagined that I was gathering spirits of different animals and insects into my body in order to survive space.

When the nurses would bring food to the patients, I thought that the foods were body parts of nasty insects so I would avoid eating. I went about a week without eating until one of the nurses brought me a plastic wrapped PB & J sandwich and some orange juice in a sealed cup. When I ate, the nurse excitedly told other nurses that she was able to get me to eat as the nurses were worried about my rapid weight-loss. I started eating normal food because I had a roommate who would eat, so I thought it was safe for me to eat as well and I was released back to the general ward.

The third time I was admitted to the hospital, I saw a couple of patients who were there during my second hospitalization at Methodist. The reason that I needed to go back to the hospital was because I went to a house party where I drank an unreasonable amount of liquor and became drunk. When I came home, I became manic from the amount of alcohol and I wasn't able to sleep and eat. I realized that any alcohol or lack of regular sleep leads me into manic state.

During the third time in the mental hospital, I couldn't sleep properly and I would say all sorts of crazy things during the group sessions. I constantly asked the doctor and nurses to be discharged from the mental hospital. Finally, when the doctor placed me on right medication, I was able to recover from my manic episodes and I was discharged from the hospital for the last time.

I am very thankful to Lifepath (Collin County MHA) for their Support when we moved in and out of insurance. I learned to accept my mental condition, decided to stay on with the treatment, and maintained regular doctor visits. It has been more than 2 years since I was hospitalized. Now I take medication regularly, manage my sleep and watch over the stress inducing factors carefully. Now I know how to reach for help when I get my episodes and cooperate taking medication to recover quickly.

3. A FATHER'S HOPE

3.1 How it all started

It was summer 2010.

Josh was in transition from 9th to 10th grade. One day, around lunch I got a call from my wife saying Josh and his sleepover friend were not responding well. Out of panic, she called 911 and they were taken to Plano Medical Center.

That evening we were told that Josh's blood test showed marijuana, and the boys were discharged with a warning from the doctor. Josh went on to narrate that he & his friend ate some brownies given by one of his friends in the neighborhood. We quickly understood that those brownies were laced with marijuana. We warned him not to take anything questionable and watch out.

I observed that Josh started sleeping too much and waking up late all through the summer. Also noted that he gradually became skinny. For a moment I thought it may be growth hormones, and nothing to be concerned about. However, I noticed him sneaking out of our home randomly and showing up at odd times with some loose excuses. I confronted him a few times when he told me he was going to a friend's home, but started going in exactly opposite direction. He started acting suspiciously from then onwards. Also, he gradually became edgy when questioned about his whereabouts when he didn't show up at a certain time.

Looking back, I realized that he was regularly getting marijuana in one form or the other through his school friends or neighborhood drug dealers. Around this time, I also noticed that he was bringing home expensive iPod or a cell phone. When questioned, he gave some excuse saying it was his friend's.

In 2011, trouble started at his high school. One afternoon, I got a call from the high school.

Upon arrival, I found that Josh was arrested on some illegal drug related charges at school and taken to Plano city jail, along with his close friend. I paid the bail and got him out. The campus police told me that it was a common occurrence when kids get hooked onto marijuana, they start doing stupid stuff to get money for marijuana.

The following year 2012, we made him move to another high school to keep away from his old friends, and hoped that perhaps he would have a new beginning. However, it was not so, as I started getting calls from the school about Joshua's behavior at the new school, and he was sent home on a couple of occasions, and in one instance he passed out in a classroom. At this time, I tried to threaten him either he quits the drug on his own, or I would forcefully admit him at a rehab facility and that he would be allowed into our home unless he completes the rehab. To which, Josh responded that I can do whatever I wish and he will fake through the program and keep doing it once he is out. It would be waste of money and effort forcing him through the rehab.

Just around that time, my company (Genesis) was not doing well and we were forced to raise more capital or close it down. I left for India in Dec 2012 to close a low interest funding option. However, it fell into indefinite delays and I had to come back in June 2013. In the meantime, things were getting worse with Joshua. Despite all of this, he was able to score well on his SAT exam and gained admission to the University of Texas at Dallas Business School.

Fall 2013

As he started his first semester, things got worse and he was barely passing his courses. During Fall 2013, one evening cops came to our home and picked up Joshua saying he threatened to commit suicide, as reported by his supposed girlfriend. He was admitted at Green Oaks Rehab facility in Dallas, and was released after 24 hours. Towards the end of the semester, he was admitted at Green Oaks for a psychotic breakdown at home. After 4 days of monitoring, he was released. When he was at home, he was constantly looking for money to buy marijuana.

When we refused to help him, he wanted to sell his old clothes and shoes.

He was taken to Green Oaks again towards month end, but they released him after a couple of days. On the evening of December 31st, he took off and ended up at a four-star hotel in downtown Dallas. On Jan 1st at noon, I got a call from Dallas city jail as he was arrested for public intoxication the night before. When he was home, he was constantly on the lookout for money.

Once Josh turned 18, these hospitalizations became a nightmare for us as the hospitals would not inform us of the details of his condition without his permission. This legal right to privacy put us in a bind often and we always felt extremely helpless until he called us.

Spring 2014

Things got rough starting January. I had to force him to Green Oaks again due to his erratic behavior as he stopped going to school, but constantly indulged in marijuana. The first time, the doctors formally evaluated him and said he was bipolar, schizophrenic and a few others. Once he started seeing the psychiatrist and taking his medication regularly, he started doing well. He started working at Subway and showed responsibility to be accountable. He registered for summer classes and completed them well.

Just around this time, we decided to sell off Genesis as an acquisition of another solar company and our relaunch plan went into limbo. By this time, I had not taken a pay check for 2 years, had consumed a small pension account from Texas Instruments, and started depleting my 401K fast. One of the Genesis investors wired me some money to keep me afloat until we went through a formal sale or a merger settlement. This put enormous financial strain on our family.

Fall 2014

From Fall 2014, Josh started driving to school. Within no time, with renewed freedom he started associating with friends who were into drugs. Between him and his friends, he started getting speeding tickets and running into law enforcement one way or the other. Every month he was getting a ticket, or getting arrested for a misdemeanor. I stopped keeping track of his tickets, and he was barely at home during day or night. Even routine things were slowly turning into tense situation at home, especially when we received a call from Josh, we never knew what would happen that day or the next.

3.2 Highway to California

Obviously, he didn't complete the fall semester. Things were slowly spiraling out of control. On the morning of Dec 18th, he said he wanted to go to California and work with a rapper. He barely had $50 in his pocket, but took off. Josh called me around 7pm saying that he got stranded without gas near Sweet Water, Texas. It was about 300 miles west on I20. I put some money in his account and told him to get gas, eat and head back. He said he would do it, but ended up sleeping in his car that night.

During this time, he started asking if a certain rapper celebrity (WK) came and knocked on our door for Josh. When we told Josh that WK was a well-established rapper and he never came to our home, he started blaming us saying that we didn't open the door and that we let him go. Every hour or so, he started with the same questions or conversation and started blaming us for not welcoming WK into our home. We didn't understand what was happening and what it meant. It was a nightmare to us.

Next day, Josh called me around 3PM saying that his ATM got hacked and he needed some money to buy food and gas. Later, around 5pm, I got a call from him again saying that he lost his car, and gave the phone to a local sheriff. The local sheriff from Putnam, TX explained what he thought just took place there. Putnam is a really small town off of I-20 before Abilene, and the railway track was at least half a mile away from the highway. He said that Josh was lucky to survive as his car got stalled on a railway track and in no time a freight train came through, crashed his car and pushed it into a ditch next to the tracks. The car became a complete wreck.

Some background on the car. When we gave the Honda Accord to him, it was in a pristine condition. During his wild rides with his friends, they messed up the Honda's driver's side door and it stopped closing properly. So, he and his friends completely shut it off with heavy duct tape such that he entered the driver's seat from the passenger side. This thought sent chills through me thinking how did he get out of the car as the train approached his car. Only God's hand protected him as there was no one else in the vicinity to testify how he got out. And he wasn't in a condition to explain the details how it happened.

The sheriff told me that he would drop off Josh at a nearby shop and I could come and pick him up. Immediately I took off for the 4 hour drive. When I reached the shop location, Josh wasn't there. I contacted the police and they came looking for him. Someone nearby pointed that Josh was looking for a ride to go to the

Greyhound bus station at Abilene, which was another 30 miles further west.

When I arrived at the Greyhound station, I saw Josh standing there, totally out of place and smoking. It was cold 40 degrees F and windy, but he wasn't wearing any jacket other than a long sleeved t-shirt. He didn't acknowledge me as he was in his own world. I goaded him for over an hour to go back home with me. After some time, I convinced him to eat and we had a Subway sandwich. The passengers who were listening to our conversation also pleaded with him to go home. A couple of people appeared to lecture him as they narrated their own lives of mistakes and misery. Josh wouldn't budge.

Then he tried to get on a bus going to El Paso without a ticket. The Greyhound called police and two policemen came and warned Josh not to do it again. It was beyond midnight and it was getting colder. Then came a bus going to LA, and Josh sneaked on it while I was on phone with my wife, Mary.

3.3 The Taylor County Interception

Then I realized he was not in right mind, and didn't seem to understand what he was doing. I could see that this might turn into a potentially life-threatening situation if he were to be dropped off somewhere, without money and shelter. If I didn't stop him, things could get worse! Please note – at this time we didn't have a clue about mental health issues tied to drugs.

I called the cops and informed them to take Josh away for a few days. However, they said they could keep him at best 24 hrs. only as it was a public nuisance issue and they had no grounds to hold him any longer. I said ok and I would come pick him up the next day morning. It was just past 2 am. I turned heater on and slept in my SUV. I arrived at Taylor County jail around 9:30am thinking I had whole day, but they already had let him out and I saw Josh was sitting on a cement bench in front of the jail.

When I approached him, he didn't want to leave, instead he said WK was coming to pick him up. It appeared like he was constantly posting on WK Facebook page and thinking that he was communicating with him. It was just one-sided postings, and there was no response from WK admin. I realized a deeply troubling pattern of thought was developing with Josh, but I could not figure it out. We didn't know about the delusions of grandeur, or other hallucinations, tied to drugs use.

I parked in such a way that I could see him and stayed inside the vehicle whole day. He would not even sit inside the vehicle. I brought him lunch, and he ate it. From time to time, he came to the vehicle to get his phone charged and then walked back to the bench. By 4pm, the weather started turning cold and it was becoming unbearable outside. Finally, Josh came to the vehicle and asked me to drive around to a place where WK would be waiting for him. I obliged and took him around, and he made me stop at a furniture shop parking lot and started cursing me in vilest terms. All the while I could see that he was getting frustrated not getting any response from WK. He got off and walked away. It was almost dark outside.

I didn't know what my next step would be. I thought unless he learns some hard lesson he is not going to come around. So, I told Mary that I was coming home, and she started pleading with me not to leave him there. She said, do whatever it takes and wait until he changes his mind. I drove almost 30 miles East and stopped at a gas station, got some gas and walked over to Chicken Express for dinner.

While I was eating dinner, I got a call from Josh again, and this time he handed the phone to an Abilene cop. The cop told me that unless someone picks up Josh they will be forced to take him for loitering and unruly conduct. Immediately I drove back to the vicinity where I dropped him off earlier, and I saw that cops had already detained him in a police cruiser. When he saw me, he got into the SUV without any protest, and I started heading back home.

Instead of being thankful, he went on a vile rant and became very aggressive towards me verbally. It was as if hell was unleashed through his anger, words and expressions. Again, he went into the blame game saying that I was taking him away from his music partner WK. I bought him dinner on the way, and he relented a little after the dinner and slept off the rest of the 4-hour journey. We reached home around 2am.

Once inside the home, he unleashed his anger and verbal abuse towards his mom and me. For the first time, I sensed something of a dark force operating through him, and was somewhat concerned for the well-being of Josh and our own lives. He slept on our living room couch. I told my younger son to lock his door, and we locked our door too! By that time, Mary, hardly slept the night before, was going through panic attacks. I was totally exhausted and I slept it off.

3.4 The Alternate World

For the next few days, Josh started acting erratically while constantly smoking and berating us. He was constantly posting on WK's Facebook page and expecting WK to show up at any time to pick him up. After 2 days, he packed up all his stuff, set aside his high-power amplifier and guitars near front door. He was barely sleeping and eating, but on constant alert for WK arriving at any moment. One day morning, he moved his stuff outside near the curb and stood there for hours and hours. Then he brought his stuff back inside towards evening. Even then he was getting frustrated, not hearing from WK.

On 4th day, he downsized all his stuff to two bags, and asked me to drop him off at DFW airport close to 3am. Josh told me that WK is coming to the terminal C the following day to pick him up. However, nothing really happened at the airport for next 48 hours. On the evening of the third day, just past midnight, he called me saying that he took a taxi and went to friend's house in Carrolton and he needed some cash to pay off the taxi. I went and picked him up, and he sounded somewhat thankful.

A day later, he asked me to drop him off at the same friend's place. I dropped him off early evening, and close to midnight he called me saying his friend wasn't home. It was freezing cold that night. I went to pick him up, but didn't find him there. And when he called he sounded barely coherent and couldn't give me any address. I got anxious and started driving around the whole neighborhood. After an hour, somehow, he made it back to the place where I dropped him off earlier, and found him to be shivering. He may have been on the verge of hypothermia! As soon as he got into the vehicle, he felt relieved and dozed off.

3.5 The Mental Health Warrant

The next day, he started verbally abusive ranting and shrieking from time to time. His obsession with WK grew steadily and he started treating us as if we were impediments to his success in the music industry. Things started turning tense not knowing what he would do at any moment. That evening, I am not sure what agitated him, but he started taunting me and lit up the bible in our living room. Knowing his mental state, I put out the fire and called 911. The cops came and spoke to him.

I suggested the cops take him to Green Oaks again, but they explained that they cannot do anything unless he is an imminent danger to himself or others. Since he is an adult, the only way to force him to a hospital is to get a mental health warrant. That was the first time I ever heard about a Mental Health Warrant!

The following morning, I rushed to Collin County Justice of Peace (JP) court and filed for a Mental Health Warrant with a detailed write up of Josh's condition. By afternoon, I went before the judge and had to explain the history of Josh's situation and the judge granted a Mental Health Warrant.

For those who know how the mental health warrant works, this is redundant information. Steps to procure a Mental Health Warrant are listed on the last page of this book. For others, here it is briefly.

Once a person is an adult, parents or a guardian cannot force their will on the person even if they are sick. i.e., we could not make Josh to go hospital unless he went voluntarily. When the person is incapacitated, or seeks to harm himself or others, the caretaker goes before the judge and files for a mental health warrant, which gives a legal right to police to apprehend the person and take him or her to an appropriate mental health provider. Once the person is taken over to the mental health provider, the person can be released upon the certification of an attending doctor only!

I stopped at a church parking lot near our home and called the cops explaining that I had a mental health warrant for Josh. Within 5 minutes, two police cruisers showed up. I explained the situation and handed over the mental health warrant to them. They asked if Josh was violent, or if we had fire arms inside our home. And I answered 'no' for both questions.

I parked inside the garage and the police showed up at the front door within 2 minutes. When I let them in, they came to Josh and explained that they need to take him to hospital as they had Mental Health Warrant. Josh obliged without any resistance, but the police still had to put cuffs on him and walk him out through the front door. They took him to Green Oaks again and handed off the paper work.

Prior to this, Josh was arrested a few times for misdemeanors, but seeing him arrested in our home with hands behind his back was the most heartbreaking thing. It was too emotional to put it in words. As things developed, this was not the first or the last time, he had to be taken to the hospital by police several times. Each time, it was a heart-breaking experience!

I requested that Green Oaks keep him there for a long-term observation and rehab. Since Green Oaks doesn't permit more than a week of observation, they recommended Terrell State Hospital (TSH), which is 80 miles East of Dallas. Upon a formal written request, Green Oaks moved Josh to TSH. Once he was moved to TSH, we visited him regularly.

He did well as long as he was under supervision and taking the medication.

A word on parental and doctor limitations. Since Josh was an adult, we could not force our will on how long he should be kept there. Even the attending doctor was getting push back from Texas mental health law, as well as the insurance company, to let him out once he was back to normal state. So, they wanted to release him after 2 weeks. I had to go before a mental health court within Collin County and request additional monitoring. However, he was released after 3 weeks, and was put on a daily medication with periodic visits to a psychiatrist.

3.6 NAMI – A Coping Mechanism

A social worker and a nurse at TSH recommended that we connect with a local National Alliance on Mental Illness (NAMI) support group. For the first time, Mary and I attended a NAMI session at a Custer Road Methodist church. NAMI has two types of support groups – (a) to help the people caring (parents, loved ones), and (b) to help those who are going through mental health or other addiction issues.

In some cultures, mental illness or addiction issues are seen as shameful things and the caretakers tend to bottle it up as they don't receive any support from family members, or the community. This leads to hopelessness and they try to manage it using their own limited understanding or means. This can take huge toll on their own mental well-being, and in the process subject other family members to the trauma of this uncharted area in their lives. This is where NAMI plays a big role as a community support group to help the caretakers, and the afflicted.

For the first time, we realized we are not alone in this journey. Once we were seated with nearly 25 people, the facilitator updated the group on recent mental health legislation and the available resources. Then opened the floor for sharing. Some were parents, some were siblings, and some were grandparents, but all of us were in the same boat in dealing with a person afflicted with a mental health or an addiction issue.

As we narrated how it got started and where we were then, it was a relief to hear similar symptoms in others, especially delusions of grandeur, manic personality, and extreme mood swings. The marijuana is like a gateway drug, which opens the door for other hard drugs later on. People get carried away with thinking that they will just experiment with marijuana and enjoy it, but it doesn't stop there. The euphoric high they get becomes routine after a while, and they crave other hard drugs. From there, it is downhill only. When they stop the drug, they go through depression from withdrawals. Depending on the type of drug, some withdrawals are worse than others.

We encouraged Josh to attend the other group, which encourages those who are coming out of addiction issues. However, he did not show further interest to attend and we did not force it on him. I highly recommend NAMI local groups to caretakers as it is a genuinely helpful avenue to share your heart openly. People learn from each other what worked and what didn't, and develop a network of support. NAMI also helps you to connect with local city and county mental health options for emergencies and other pro bono services.

3.7 The God Comfort

When everything is said and done, you are all alone as the days drag into weeks, and weeks turn to months, without an end in sight. One has to find a way to process the challenge on hand and be able to move on for the sake of the family and be sane. It is not easy to move things to a side of brain and continue as if everything is ok.

For some, it is regret or blame game that dominate their lives that they haven't intervened early on. Why people responsible in their life didn't intervene to do what was necessary, perhaps to avert this disaster. Either one will make life more burdensome, and causes other internal trauma.

NAMI, friends and other concerned people in your life make a difference. They will give time to listen and counsel, and even pray for comfort & wisdom. As soon as I realized there is only so much I could do and understand my own limitations, the sooner I found my sense of true comfort knowing that God is always there for me, and my family. I have a personal track record of God's love and His faithfulness in my own life.

When I thought about how much I loved Josh despite his mistakes, God reminded me of a higher form of love. Love that is more than that of a mother! And God inscribed Josh's name on His own hands. What more was God not willing to do to bring back our Josh? Nothing. The Lord God will restore Josh from the brink of destruction.

"Can a woman forget her nursing child,
And not have compassion on the son of her womb?
Surely, they may forget, Yet I will not forget you.
See, I have inscribed you on the palms of My hands;"
Isaiah 49:15-16a

This assurance from the Bible became my confidence that God is in-charge of Josh's life and we just have to do whatever it takes – to be there for him, love him and assure him of God's love and purpose through his life.

There were times we could not do anything other than pray and go to bed. Every now and then I used to go to Josh's bed room and pray for him to be fully restored. The Lord did not disappoint us.

3.8 Restored from the Edge of Abyss

The way things were spiraling out of control, I was preparing myself that anything could happen. Perhaps God may call him home early. I counted at least 3 different occasions where Josh went to the point of life and death. Later Josh revealed another 2 more occasions where he could have breathed his last. Through all these uncontrollable circumstances, the Lord kept him intact. He did suffer some physical consequences for his choices and the mental illness.

Just when he was released from TSH, a close family friend's daughter passed away due to a brain tumor. Josh and her were of the same age group and both were at UTD. She exhibited robust faith in the midst of suffering. When Josh saw what happened to her, it affected him somewhat and he appeared to reconsider his decisions. But soon, he went back to his old ways.

Summer 2015

He took summer classes and completed them. Just before fall, we bought a pre-owned Volvo S45 sport sedan for his commute to school. As soon as he sat in the driver seat, he drove to downtown Dallas to attend a concert. Very quickly, things went downhill again. Between him and his friend (without a driver's license), they drove the car to the ground. After fixing the car, he went back to the wild side again, which resulted in multiple speeding and other traffic violation tickets.

One morning, Josh and his friend took off to go to CA again, but got stranded again at Abilene and came back after a couple of days. He came and parked in front of our home, but didn't come inside. After sometime he just drove off into the night. The next afternoon, I got a call from Josh saying he was arrested for possession. His car got towed away that night and I picked up the car. They completely trashed the vehicle inside and outside.

I decided not to bail out Josh, and told him to stay there for some time. When the detention center realized no one was coming to bail him out, they decided to let him go on his own cognizance. When they released him, instead of calling me he started wandering in the streets on his own. He called me next day at about 4 am from a gas station and I picked him up. He seemed pretty rough with some injuries and totally disheveled.

During conversation, he revealed that he got into a fight with an inmate. I understood that is one way to keep himself bullied by others. Essentially, you put on a show and take on someone to make a statement to the rest of the crowd not to mess with him.

While at home, he was totally out of control. He went out whenever he wanted to and came home at random times in the night. Due to my own financial challenges, I did not indulge him with money to buy drugs.

One day he left home and stopped answering the phone. When he didn't show up for more than 24 hours, I filed for a missing person report. Since Plano PD already has his number, somehow, they called and checked to see if he was ok. He came home that evening quite angry. He looked really bad with poor hygiene and shabby in dress. I learned later on that he was with some friends who are into hard drugs at a Motel 6 close to our home.

When he was home, it was constant trauma to Mary not knowing what he would do next. At the same time, we had to watch over Jonathan, so that he was not affected by this dysfunctional environment. Josh drove the car again unto the ground and it got stalled in front of our home.

3.9 Fateful Fall 2015

He didn't register for Fall semester. I realized he was not in a right state of mind, so I thought he would settle down skipping one semester. But his erratic behavior continued.

On Oct 05, I came home late in the evening. Mary called me on the way and said Josh was up to something in his room when she smelled some strong smoke coming out. I tried to understand what he was doing and calm down the situation. It looked like he meddled with some hard drugs and he was really high.

Things got escalated quickly and he started cursing me in a very demeaning way. When approached him to calm him down, the situation worsened quickly. Somehow, he got hold of a steak knife and came at me threatening to kill himself if we called the cops. Sensing the gravity of the matter, I told Mary and Jonathan to exit through the garage door and stand outside. As soon as they were out, I also quickly exited and Josh closed the door hard behind me.

Joshua quickly locked all the doors. I sensed that he would do something to harm himself or to the house. So, I called 911 immediately. Police showed up in a few minutes and I explained the situation. They saw him on the front porch smoking, and when they approached him, he ran inside and locked the door. The police asked us to fill out a case form, and write a detailed statement on the situation. While I was filling out the paper work, I saw that a SWAT team had arrived. Unbeknown to us, apparently Josh also called 911 and said that he had bombs at our home, and posted some expletively against the police.

All this raised alarm, and they dispatched the SWAT team. In his delusions and manic condition, he didn't know what he was setting himself against. Later we came to know that he was trying suicide by cops.

It was about 11:30pm. I sensed some impending danger if Josh didn't comply and come out peacefully. The Plano PD cordoned off our neighborhood street on all four sides. They started asking more probing questions: "Did we have fire arms at home? Had Josh bought any materials related to bomb making?" They assigned a negotiator to communicate with Josh. A family friend (pastor Jon) and his wife came and stayed with us during this critical time.

As the SWAT team started probing Josh's access to guns or other explosive materials, I had to explain that he had mental illness due to drug use and he needed help. Perhaps he was attempting a suicide as my wife saw white crushed powder on kitchen counter top and on the floor in his room. I told them, if necessary, shoot his feet to take custody of him. Later I understood, in such a scenario, the only outcome would be to bring out the person in a body bag! This thought sends chills to my spine even today. All we could do was pray and wait.

As the night was dragging on without any progress, the Plano PD deployed a communication center with all types of supplies for the people at the site. It was close to 2PM, and I prompted Mary and Jonathan to go to the pastor's home and I stayed behind in a police cruiser. With all the exhaustion, I was dozing off from time to time.

Somewhere close to 5AM, I heard several shots fired and I woke up fearing something had happened to Josh. After a few minutes, one of the cops came by and informed me that they caught hold of Josh. Finally, close to 6AM, I was allowed to step off the cruiser and go check our home.

As I walked to the front of our home, I saw strewn blood-soaked clothes and other personal belongings of Josh in our front lawn. All the windows were broken and the house was without power. My front door was completely broken down and barely hanging on the hinges. As I tried to enter the house, a very strong whiff of tear gas hit me hard that I had to jump out of the room to the patio. I had never been exposed to tear gas in my life and I understood why police use it to disperse the crowds. Our home looked like a war zone inside with almost all windows broken through, and furniture toppled or strewn all over.

3.10 Is He Alive?

An elderly gentleman from opposite house, who watched the unfolding events from his living room, thought Josh was dead as he didn't see any movement when they brought him out in a body bag and laid him on front lawn in early morning hours. He came running concerned as I was standing outside and asked me why the police had to shoot him. At this time, I broke down and started crying, and my mind went in all directions. I didn't know whether the police had told me the truth. At this time, my next-door neighbors (Susan and Tim) approached me. They suggested we immediately go to Plano Medical Center to see Josh.

When we arrived at the Medical Center, I was not allowed to see Josh saying he was in police custody. I wanted to make sure that Josh was OK. Both the nurses and the supervisor did not give me a definitive answer as to how he was doing. After 30 min or so, a social worker came by who was attending to Josh. She was the first one to confirm that Josh was alive and fully sedated due to several fractures, etc. Hearing those words brought full relief to me, and I started processing what may have happened during the SWAT intervention.

Apparently, the hospital performed surgery the same day on his shattered right knee cap, and his fingers. They had to insert metal structures to repair the shattered knee cap.

By the next day, Josh was moved to the Collin County Detention Center. Plano PD put a restraining order on Josh as a minor (his brother) was still at home. And I was asked not to contact him. However, after getting some legal counsel, I started adding some cash to his commissary account weekly so he could buy supplies.

Our house was uninhabitable, and we were moved to an extended-stay apartment and the insurance crew started working on the home. It took nearly two and half months to salvage our stuff and fix our house. They had to throw off quite a bit of stuff infused with tear gas, repair all the walls where tear gas cannisters landed, replace carpet, all inside doors & all windows, repaint inside walls, and replace AC plenum. We moved back into the house close to Christmas 2015.

Josh started calling us (collect calls). Mary took the third call and assured him that we loved him and planned to see him soon. In early January, I went to see him and Mary stayed behind as it was still traumatic to her. He was kept in the isolation ward, which is the most secure place inside.

As I waited near a metal gate, they brought him with full shackles. He looked ok and smiled the moment he saw me. I could not touch him but was able to speak to him over the intercom phone. I prayed and encouraged him, but left with a heavy heart. I didn't know what would happen to him, as I understood they booked him under second degree felony, which could mean 4 to 10 years prison time.

Mary and I both visited him next time, and it was really hard for Mary to see him in that state. Through a family friend who had a brother with similar issues, we understood that we could make an appeal to the judge since Josh was still in school at UT Dallas. I documented all the events that led up to that fateful night, and wrote an appeal letter to Collin Count District Attorney. Then Josh's public defense attorney contacted me and advised us to meet with him at the McKinney court house. I suggested that Josh should be released under some type of probation as he needed mental help, not jail time, to recoup and get back to school.

The prosecutor and the defense attorney came to an agreement that they would put Josh on 6-year probation. If he stayed sober without any further violations, the charges would not stick to his record. And Josh was released on Feb 12, 2016. He was assigned to be under a probation officer for monthly check-in.

This is what I learned later putting together all the events that took place that fateful night.

Josh inhaled some hard substance and some crushed ibuprofen powder, and it put him over the edge, which led to the escalation of the events when I arrived home. He did not eat anything, but he was thinking he would be shot as he heard the SWAT team blaring on the loud speaker for him to come out. So, he put on multiple layers of clothing thinking they would shoot him. He was attempting suicide by cops.

A robotic arm completely pulled off Josh's bedroom window. Even then he did not budge to come out despite the horrific tear gas inside. Then the SWAT team broke the front door and enter the house. They shot several rounds of rubber bullets at Josh to take him down. In the process, his right knee was knocked out and he suffered fractures on the fingers and upper body.

After he was released, we went to two different hospitals to collect his surgery videos and reports. Plano Med Center worked on his right knee and fixed with it metal structures, and another hospital operated on his fingers. Even then they could not fix his right-hand ring finger as the knuckle was completely gone. It does not fold like other fingers even today!

3.11 Road to Recovery

It was not an easy path to get back to normalcy for Josh. The trauma showed up in multiple ways, but he registered for the summer classes in 2016. Even then he stumbled a few times, which led to few hospitalizations. However, he did not give up, but continued with his schooling.

With the love and support from the family, Josh made good progress and finally graduated receiving Bachelors in Business Administration with finance major in Aug 2020. Throughout this ordeal till present, his younger brother Jonathan has been a great support to both Josh and their mother.

Another accomplishment to his credit, he quit smoking completely by early 2021. He accepted his mental health condition, stays on the medication and follows up with his regular visits to the doctor, thus managing his mental health condition.

Even writing this book is part of an outreach, he and I discussed knowing what this means to loved ones. Now he is open to share and perhaps change the minds of those who are still struggling with the addiction.

3.12 Cultural and Family Background

The addiction and mental health issues are trans-cultural, trans-ethnic and trans-racial issues. However, the people dealing with these issues fall into certain predilections that are all too common from their family background.

In walking down this path, I have seen that cultural and ethnic (family) background plays a role. One cannot help but learn to deal with it as they are bound by certain stigmas and fears.

For example, having come from Indian (South Asian) cultural background, our default position is to suffer silently out of fear of shame and stigma. Each racial/ethnic background deals with it in a way, which comes naturally to them.

Once you overcome the fear and stigma issues and focus on the end goal, which is to see your loved one getting better, you will do yourself a favor. By not subjecting yourself to certain imaginary expectations from your family or community, you help yourself significantly, and experience less stress.

Sometimes, the loved ones become the enablers unwittingly, out of fear or other reasons. If you're the enabler through manipulation, you need to seek counsel and get out of that mode if you really want to see your loved-one on the mend.

4. HOPE AGAINST HOPE

For those who never travelled down this path, it is somewhat hard to process the facts. There was a time I thought Josh might not make it, and I mentally prepared myself for a fateful end. It was that serious. There is no sugar coating the reality.

I counted at least three different incidents that took him close to death, besides the SWAT incident. Josh himself recalled another two more incidents, which put him close to death.

All of us have to process grief or pain in a way that works for us, which is often referred to as a coping mechanism. AA or NAMI groups really help to vent and share things which help in so many ways, especially learning from others what helped them to come to the other side.

Even with so many people around you and the support groups you can lean on, at the end of the day it is you who have to walk through this unknown territory. Frustration and hopelessness are routine parts of life, and it feels like a never-ending pain. The nature of these issues may not have a clear ending, which we prefer to see, but can at least we can see a path of progress that leads towards healing.

4.1 The Lasting Hope

I came to know Jesus during my college days, and the personal relationship with the Lord helped me tremendously in navigating through life challenges.

For me, it goes back to Josh's childhood and how many times I laid my hands praying over him again and again. During prayer, God reminded me often that He is in-charge of his life more than anyone else. Josh believed in Jesus and got baptized when he was a pre-teen. He has that sensitivity towards God and prayer, however he denied it or walked away from it. God used several scriptural promises to strengthen me and assure peace when everything looked bleak.

Recently Josh recommitted his life to the Lord Jesus and got baptized. We thank God for His grace upon both our sons Josh and Jonathan.

Old Testament patriarch, Abraham persevered in faith when he did not see any evidence that what he believed would come to pass.

Abraham, **against all hope, believed in hope**, *that he might become the father of many nations, according to that which had been spoken, "So shall thy seed be."*
Romans 4:18 (SV) (Emphasis mine)

In the natural world, he was without a child of his own flesh, but God promised him that, *"I have made thee a father of many nations"*. It is impossible to believe such a grand-standing promise when there was nothing in the natural world to back it up. Abraham could count on what he saw in the natural world, his advanced age where he cannot father a child and that of his wife Sara, who is well past childbearing age, or believe in God that is Sovereign Almighty and He can make things happen to him despite all the physical limitations.

When it is boiled down, do I believe that God would take a totally messed up life, such as Josh, and bring something good out of his life? I choose to believe that God is well able to do this, and this gave me great assurance and peace.

4.2 Peace or Stress

People bottle up an unusual amount of stress when their loved ones go through these situations. It often results in terrible emotional trauma, which sometimes manifests as panic attacks, or other illness. This does not stop, but becomes an ongoing trauma to deal with. Often times, it came to whether I could sleep through the night. I found myself sleeping like a baby, worry-free.

If you are fed up with religion or the church, I understand. People messed up the religion and the church, but Jesus is perfect and He is always there for you and me.

Don't sacrifice your relationship with the Heavenly Creator due to some hurts or misunderstanding with religious people. It is not too late to trust Him. He will transform your life for the better. This decision alone makes a world of difference in going forward.

When I look back, I could see God's promise to give peace to those who put their trust in Him. His peace guarded my heart and mind, and allowed me to go through this period with ease. I knew I didn't have it within me to handle the end-less trauma, pressure and stress, but I thank God for His peace and strength.

"You will keep him in perfect peace, whose mind is stayed on You, because he trusts in You."
Isaiah 26:3

If there is a way, we can make it through our own strength, we will do it. These things test you to uttermost and drain you out. Unlike a temporary setback, these addiction related issues take their toll and even the best support from family and friends, we will fall short of the peace and strength we need.

This is where God's strength becomes ours if we choose to trust Him, and roll over our burdens to Him for He sustains us. These promises often made me look up to the Lord and receive much needed comfort.

"Your words are what sustain me; they are food to my hungry soul. They bring joy to my sorrowing heart and delight me. How proud I am to bear your name, O Lord." Jeremiah 5:16

"I lay down and slept; I awoke, for the Lord sustained me." Psalm 3:5

"Cast your burden on the Lord, And He shall sustain you; He shall never permit the righteous to be moved." Psalm 55:22

You can always second-guess someone's opinion, but you can never go wrong trusting the Lord. If anything, this relationship with God fills you with joy and strength to carry on with a positive outlook.

4.3 On-going Journey

As I write this, I am very confident that God settled down Josh with a positive and thankful attitude. He had been sober for the last 5+ years. I am sure God will help redeem his lost years too.

I encouraged Josh to be open and share his experience so others could feel hope and get off from this destructive path. That's what prompted us to document this journey.

Sometimes others write off our beloved ones. Sometimes they give up on themselves and in doing so go to extremes to harm themselves. Sometimes we write them off as a lost cause, but God can turn around any situation. He can handle all our trials and bring beauty from the ashes. This is what we see in Isa. 61:3.

"To console those who mourn in Zion,
To give them beauty for ashes,
The oil of joy for mourning,
The garment of praise for the spirit of heaviness;
That they may be called trees of righteousness,
The planting of the Lord, that He may be glorified."
　　　　Isaiah 61:3 (Emphasis mine)

If you are the loved one on this lonely road, please know that God loves and cares for you. He is willing to be your burden-bearer and walk with you. Trust Him for you have nothing to lose. God bless you.

4.4 It's Not Too Late!

Whether you are the one who is struggling with addiction issues, or you are their caregiver, both need God's help to come out of this situation intact. It' Not Too Late! Despite collateral damage and terrible consequences, God will restore you to normalcy over a period of time.

God will bring beauty from the ashes of your life (Isaiah 61:3). The society and even some in the community may write you off as a lost cause, but God loves you and restores you.

My own experience and others who leaned on God were never let down, and it will be true of anyone who will put their trust in Lord Jesus Christ during life's most challenging time.

Epilogue

If you are reading this book because you are on this destructive path, it is Not Too late to reconsider your decisions and get help. In the long scheme of life, this will be a small blot once you get over it. You are not an island; You are hurting so many people in your family because of your self-destructive path. They are trying to help you, not take away your fun, but you have to reach out and take advantage of it. You can do it and by God's grace you will see a better side of life.

If you are an afflicted family member whose loved one is going through an addiction or self-inflicted harm, our encouragement is for you to stay the course. First, take care of your own health, especially mental well-being by seeking a support group such as NAMI or church counselors who understand addiction and mental illness as biological brain disorders.

It is like a marathon and it takes toll on both the person on the destructive path and the loved ones who are standing by to help. Both need God, prayers and encouragement. God bless you both.

Resources

1. www.nami.org National Alliance on Mental Illness
2. suicidepreventionlifeline.org/ National Suicide Prevention Line; 800-273-TALK (8255)
3. Contact MHMR or Mental Health Authority in your county for resources.

Procuring a Mental Health Warrant

Please check your respective State and County laws where to go to procure it. In Collin County, Texas, the Mental Health Warrant is issued by the local Justice of Peace Court (JP Court).

1) Any able-bodied family member, who is a caregiver, can request a Mental Health Warrant. It is preferable for a father or mother, or a sibling, to request it.
2) The JP court is usually a walk-in place during week days, where the clerk would provide an application for a Mental Health Warrant.
3) Once the application is filled in and turned it over to the clerk, they will schedule a hearing within 1-3 hours, the same day.
4) A JP Court judge will review the application and cross examine the applicant to ensure the case is valid and the cause is justified.
5) If the Judge finds it reasonable, he/she will issue the Mental Health Warrant, and the clerk will give you a signed copy for enforcement.